BEACH HOUSES

FOR YOUR HOME

BEACH HOUSES

JIM KEMP

FRIEDMAN/FAIRFAX

PUBLISHERS

DEDICATION

To the memory of William B. Stewart, who enjoyed the beach more than anyone I've known.

ACKNOWLEDGMENTS

Many thanks to all of the people at Michael Friedman Publishing Group who worked on this book, especially Reka Simonsen, Sarah Storey, and Meredith Miller.

A FRIEDMAN/FAIRFAX BOOK

Library of Congress Cataloging-in-Publication data available upon request.

ISBN 1-56799-731-7

Editor: Reka Simonsen
Art Director: Jeff Batzli
Designer: Meredith Miller
Photography Editor: Sarah Storey

Color separations by Fine Arts Repro House Co., Ltd.
Printed in Hong Kong by Midas Printing Limited.

1 3 5 7 9 10 8 6 4 2

For bulk purchases and special sales, please contact:
Friedman/Fairfax Publishers
Attention: Sales Department
15 West 26th Street
New York, New York 10010
212/685-6610   FAX 212/685-1307

Visit our website:
http://www.metrobooks.com

Table of Contents

INTRODUCTION

Picture your dream beach retreat. Is it a warm and welcoming traditional design with a nice wide front porch and wicker chairs and a swing? Perhaps you prefer a striking modern design with sharp angles, sparingly furnished with pieces in the latest contemporary style?

In either case, there's nothing quite as nice as a home by the sea, whether it's a weekend getaway or a year-round house. People have lived by the sea since the beginning of recorded history. Influential Romans built their vacation villas along the coast. The royal families of Europe retreated to the seashore to enjoy rest and relaxation. The barons of industrial-age North America built huge houses, ironically called cottages, in exclusive enclaves such as Newport, Rhode Island.

A vacation house by the sea was not solely a perk for the rich. Middle- and working-class families built or bought more modest beach houses, many of which still exist and give seashore towns their friendly and appealing character. At the peak of their popularity thirty years ago, these small houses stood cheek-by-jowl on sidestreets near the beach. Today many of them are being renovated or spruced up to satisfy more modern tastes and the challenges of today's busy lifestyles.

Opposite: Looking as if it has been there forever, this beach house basks in the sunset of yet another perfect day. Built on solid piers, the house stands as a lone sentry, patiently awaiting the return of summer. **Above:** The beach is the perfect place to linger and soak up beautiful views such as this exquisite sunset. Indeed, some form of sand-free outdoor activity area is virtually de rigueur these days. Besides providing a place to enjoy the ever-changing view, a deck greatly increases usable living space in warm weather. It can be the site of outdoor grilling and dining, an auxiliary sitting area, and a space for entertaining large groups. For the money, it is one of the best beach-house investments you can make.

Beach-house ownership, however, has lost none of its seductive qualities—escape from the workaday world, a beautiful setting for rest and relaxation, panoramic views of sky and sea, cooling ocean breezes, and perhaps a small garden. A beach house is a place for those you love, whether extended family or close friends. And it is a place for the things you love—from family heirlooms passed down through the generations to flea-market finds.

Beach houses assume many forms. Some are period houses remodeled to include modern conveniences. Many others are new constructions, representing a potpourri of building styles from modest cottages to historical revivals and unabashedly contemporary styles.

Decorating a beach home offers the opportunity to do things differently than you would at a full-time house. Old-fashioned trim, louvered doors, and window shutters applied to a traditional house not only create a "beachy" and pretty look, but they filter and soften the bright glare of sunlight off the water. In contemporary houses, large, geometric windows shaded by overhanging roofs visually invite the outdoors inside. Decks and patios draw family and guests to panoramic ocean views and casual alfresco dining. Covered outdoor walkways shelter adjacent rooms from burning sun and soaking rain. Adding a gazebo increases warm-weather living space.

There are as many kinds of beaches as there are styles of houses to build along the shore. For some, the word "beach" conjures up dazzling white sand and a turquoise southern sea that's pleasantly warm even after the sun sets.

Others dream of the salt-and-pepper sand and indigo ocean of a northern beach, where crisp breezes inspire driftwood bonfires. Whichever climate you favor, choose an area within a three-hour drive from your primary home or one with good airline connections. You may want to look for a locale with year-round activities, such as a nearby ski resort. Summer may be the best time of year to be at the beach, but a home at the water's edge is the perfect place to view the changing of the seasons. This book will take you on a private tour of wonderful beachside homes.

Opposite: THIS BEACH HOUSE REPRESENTS A POPULAR ARCHITECTURAL STYLE EMINENTLY SUITED FOR LIFE AT THE BEACH. THE 1970S MOVEMENT CALLED "THE NEW GEOMETRY" REVIVED A NUMBER OF ANGULAR MOTIFS, SUCH AS THE LEAN-TO ROOF OF THIS HOUSE. WHILE THE ROOF IS LOW ON THE STREET SIDE TO PRESERVE PRIVACY, IT RISES STEEPLY ON THE BEACH SIDE WHERE TWO FLOORS OF WINDOWS CAPTURE DRAMATIC VIEWS. A WOODEN STAIRWAY, SAFELY ILLUMINATED AT NIGHT, LEADS DIRECTLY DOWN TO THE SANDY SHORE.

Right: THERE'S NOTHING QUITE AS PRECIOUS AS A HUMBLE BEACH HOUSE THAT HAS BEEN IN THE FAMILY FOR GENERATIONS. IT'S COMFORTING TO KNOW THAT THE SAME BRILLIANT SUNSETS HAVE BEEN—AND WILL BE—SEEN BY GREAT-GRANDPARENTS AND GREAT-GRANDCHILDREN ALIKE FROM THE BACK PORCH. NO MATTER WHAT OTHER CHANGES OCCUR, THE PLACE WILL ALWAYS BE THERE TO BECKON YOUNG AND OLD TO ANOTHER VACATION IN THE SUN.

Left: THIS IS WHY WE COME TO THE SHORE—BEGUILING SEA, BEAUTIFUL SKY, AND A VIEW THAT EXTENDS FOREVER. TUCKED UNDER THE ROOF, THIS PORCH IS A PRIVATE SPOT FROM WHICH TO WATCH THE COMINGS AND GOINGS ALONG THE BEACH. THE FINISHING TOUCH IS THE ADDITION OF A SIMPLE WICKER CHAIR.

Right: A RUGGED WOODEN WALL GUARDS SEVERAL BEACH-SIDE HOMES FROM THE RAVAGES OF RISING WATER AND OCEAN STORMS. A SIMPLE FLIGHT OF WOODEN STEPS UNITES BEACH AND BACKYARD INTO AN ENTICING SUMMER SETTING.

Above: The entire point of a seaside home is to enjoy the warm sun and fresh breezes outside. The natural environment, gently dotted with tall pines or fields of coastal grasses and scrub trees swept by strong winds, is an irresistible magnet to the beach. Boardwalks of sun-bleached planks and a small area cleared to accommodate a chaise longue minimize the impact of the buildings on the land, preserving the beauty that initially made this site popular.

Gathering Rooms for Family and Friends

There's no doubt about it, when it's time to get away from it all, the seashore is the perfect destination. Geared for fun and relaxation, the beach is where immediate family, older and younger generations, and relatives or old friends who live far away can all meet to enjoy one another's company. The spirit of fun extends to creating a pleasing beach-house environment, too. People are free to decorate their beach retreat in virtually any way they please, from slipcover-chic to contemporary or one of the many options in between.

A traditional decorating scheme is the number one choice for year-round houses, so it's no surprise that this approach is also popular for many seaside getaways. Traditional decorating is comfortable, familiar, and offers the lovely patina of age. Old furniture and odds and ends blend together easily and well. Within this large category, today's trend is toward the cottage, refined country, and shabby-chic looks. Each of these settings invites friends and family alike to throw a living room pillow on the floor and join the conversation or linger over dinner. Soft colors—pale blues and yellows and creamy whites—make a traditional design scheme even more welcoming. Old-fashioned double-hung windows, paneled ceilings, and other architectural details catch the eye and beckon all to relax and stay a bit longer.

At the opposite end of the style scale is contemporary design. Though it has the reputation of being a cold and sterile look, the truth is far different. The contemporary

Opposite: Overscaled but understated sectional sofas come face-to-face in a living room of contemporary comfort. A sun-splashed round table stands ready for a rubber of bridge. Glass curtain walls, a hallmark of modern architecture, frame views during the day and provide lots of fresh air. The unembellished stone floor is easy to clean. Throughout, the neutral palette of white and natural wood finishes draws attention to the view of the sand and the ocean beyond.

style is enjoying renewed popularity because of the growth of the laid-back yet sophisticated California look. Whether in Cannes or Carmel, a house with the California look has uninterrupted expanses of glass on the ocean-view side, large-scale, sink-back-and-relax sofas and chairs, and sleek case goods meant specifically for storing the latest home and office equipment but few decorative accessories. Throughout, a monochromatic palette leans toward the brightest and whitest of whites. Small amounts of exposed stained or naturally finished woods—plum, berry reds, sunny yellows, or saturated blues—are favorite accent choices. The dining area is usually an extension of the kitchen. If the two are separated, it is by low kitchen counters or a pass-through. The streamlined kitchen offers work space for at least two cooks, an up-to-date arrangement of appliances, easy-care work surfaces, and a generous amount of storage space in sleek, lacquered cabinets with flat, hingeless doors. Convenient to move around in and quick to clean, the contemporary-style kitchen is designed to maximize time for enjoying the beach.

Traditional and contemporary decorating meet face-to-face in the eclectic style. This approach is an effective way to pull together various unrelated furnishings in a pleasing manner. Though it sounds simple to pull off, an eclectically decorated beach house requires a natural theme, a seashore color, or a common material to unify the diverse elements. At its best, the eclectic beach house is quite pretty: a living room upholstered and draped in

blue and white fabrics, natural finishes on various styles of wooden dining room furniture, and matching kitchen hardware and appliances.

Well suited to today's beach houses, all three styles fit seamlessly into the open-plan concept, currently the most common building format. In an open plan, public spaces—living area, dining area, and kitchen—are designed as a single unit. By eliminating the walls that would otherwise separate the three spaces, the open plan lowers costs for construction materials and labor, a savings passed along to the purchaser. The open plan also offers other benefits: unrestricted beach and ocean views and an easy flow of conversation from one area to another. The one possible drawback of the open plan—a lack of coziness—is easy and inexpensive to solve. Create a sense of separate rooms visually: paint one area slightly darker than the others or change floor treatments by placing area rugs in the living area, leaving a hardwood dining-area floor bare, and installing tile in the kitchen.

Opposite: ECHOING THE BEAUTY OF SKY AND SEA, BLUE HAS LONG BEEN A FAVORITE COLOR FOR BEACH HOUSES. IN THIS CASE, THE THEME EXTENDS TO THE UPHOLSTERY, FLAT-WOVEN AREA RUG, SIMPLE DRAPERIES, AND THE ACCESSORIES. BRIGHT WHITE WICKER AND NATURALLY FINISHED WAINSCOTING ON THE WALLS RECREATE THE COZINESS OF A TURN-OF-THE-CENTURY SUMMER COTTAGE BY THE SHORE.

Life at the seashore almost dictates casual decorating, regardless of style. Barefoot bathers track sand in and out, eliminating wall-to-wall carpeting and thick rugs as practical floor covering choices. Intense sunlight and reflections off the water fade dark, formal colors. It is generally easier to ride the wave of popular and proven beach-house decorating options—thick, durable sailcloth for upholstery, slipcovers, and drapery; loosely woven sisal carpeting; and nautical- or nature-themed accessories.

Instead of merely replacing kitchen appliances to reinforce a certain look, concentrate on cosmetic improvements. In a contemporary kitchen, replace cabinet doors with those that emphasize the look you want. Trade worn-out work surfaces for the newest solid-surfacing materials or polished granite. Skirt an old-fashioned sink to create additional storage space concealed from view. The traditional kitchen often looks better with the addition of wainscoting or beadboard paneling, and a colorful wallcovering decorated with tiny anchors or another nautical motif.

Left: WALL CUTOUTS AND VARYING CEILING HEIGHTS ALMOST ALWAYS CREATE A LIVELY INDOOR VIEW AND SOMETIMES EVEN REDUCE CONSTRUCTION COSTS. IN A CONTEMPORARY SETTING, THE OPENNESS RESULTS IN INDOOR FOCAL POINTS FORMED BY WHAT IS ESSENTIALLY VACANT SPACE. GLIDING PATIO DOORS FRAME OUTDOOR VIEWS IN TWO AND, OCCASIONALLY, THREE DIRECTIONS. UNOBTRUSIVE MODERN FURNISHINGS BLEND IMPERCEPTIBLY WITH NATURAL WOOD AND WHITE WALLS SPICED BY DARK ACCENTS.

Below: CANE AND WICKER CHAIRS FROM THE 1920S, '30S, AND '40S—COMPLETE WITH LARGE, SQUARE, FLORAL-PRINT CUSHIONS—ARE BIG NEWS AGAIN AS THE ARMCHAIR ENJOYS RENEWED POPULARITY. THESE STYLISH, TIMELESS PIECES BECOME A PLEASANT INDOOR FOCAL POINT WHEN COMBINED WITH LESS EYE-SURPRISING FURNISHINGS SUCH AS A COFFEE-TABLE TRUNK AND A ROUND OCCASIONAL TABLE. RESPONDING TO THE REVIVAL, SEVERAL FURNITURE MANUFACTURERS ARE PRODUCING NEW FURNITURE WITH THE FAMILIAR SILHOUETTE. THOUGH PRICES ARE ESCALATING, PERIOD PIECES CAN BE FOUND AT SHOPS WITH A FOCUS ON TWENTIETH-CENTURY FURNISHINGS. OF COURSE, THE BEST SOURCE STILL MAY BE GRANDMOTHER'S ATTIC.

Opposite: A FIREPLACE AND EASY ACCESS TO A PANORAMIC VIEW OUT-DOORS MAKE FOR A ROOM THAT ATTRACTS FRIENDS AND FAMILY THROUGHOUT THE YEAR. IN THIS CASE, THE OWNERS HAVE AUGMENTED THE ATTRACTIVE GLASS DOORS WITH A CHEERY DECORATIVE DETAIL—FLORAL PRINTS PUT TO GOOD USE AS CROWN MOLDING. OCEAN-INSPIRED MOTIFS WOULD ALSO BE AN EXCELLENT AND APPROPRIATE CHOICE. TO DOUBLE THE IMPACT, PAIR A DECORATIVE BORDER AND A RUG WITH RELATED MOTIFS AND COLORS. **Above:** IN THE CARIBBEAN AND OTHER YEAR-ROUND WARM AREAS, A COVERED PATIO CAN DOUBLE AS A SECONDARY LIVING AREA. LARGE-SCALE RATTAN SEATING UPHOLSTERED IN WHITE ELIMINATES THE SAD LOOK OF FADED FABRICS, WHILE EASILY REPLACEABLE THROW PILLOWS AND ACCESSORIES CONTRIBUTE SPLASHES OF BRIGHT COLOR. A PRACTICAL, UNOBTRUSIVE METAL AND GLASS COCKTAIL TABLE MAINTAINS THE LIGHT AND AIRY ATMOSPHERE. SHIELDED FROM THE TROPICAL SUN AND RAINSTORMS, THE OPEN-AIR SPACE IS TAILORED FOR ENTERTAINING. BY DAY, THE PATIO SERVES AS A COOL AND SHADY OASIS FROM THE SUN WITH VIEWS OF BEACHSIDE FUN FRAMED BY THE ARCHES. AS EVENING APPROACHES, IT GRADUALLY BECOMES MORE INTIMATE, ENCOURAGING RELAXED CONVERSATION AND BEFORE- OR AFTER-DINNER DRINKS.

Below: A NEUTRAL PALETTE RESULTS IN A COMPLETELY DIFFERENT EFFECT IN THIS LIVING ROOM THAT LOOKS OUT TO SEA. THOUGH THE TORCHÈRE, THE SKIRTED ARMCHAIR AND SOFA, AND THE SURPRISING SIGHT OF CLAPBOARD ON THE INTERIOR WALLS RECALL BEACH COTTAGES OF OLD, THIS BEACH RETREAT AT FLORIDA'S SEASIDE DEVELOPMENT IS NEW.

Above: AN ATTRACTIVE TRADITIONAL SETTING IS SURE TO DRAW FRIENDS AND FAMILY TO THE LIVING ROOM, WHERE THEY CAN SOAK UP THE ISLAND-DOTTED OCEAN VIEW. THE OLD-FASHIONED-LOOKING BAY WINDOW EXTENDS ALMOST FLOOR TO CEILING AND IS FLANKED BY MANY-PANED DOORS ON EACH SIDE. BEADBOARD AND BEAMS FORMING A DIAMOND SHAPE DRAW ATTENTION TO THE CEILING. UPHOLSTERED CHAIRS RECALL BOTH THE STICKLEY FURNISHINGS OF THE ARTS AND CRAFTS PERIOD AND THE CASUAL SEATING OF THE EARLY 1940s.

Right: SOARING TWO STORIES HIGH, A BAY-SHAPED, CONTEMPORARY LIVING AREA IS FLOODED WITH LIGHT THROUGH TALL WINDOWS, WHICH ALSO FRAME AN EXPANSIVE VIEW OF SEA AND SKY. THE BAY IS EMPHASIZED BY A BUILT-IN BANQUETTE THAT BRINGS PEOPLE TOGETHER AROUND A SIMPLE COFFEE TABLE. WHEN ADDITIONAL SEATING IS CALLED FOR, THE OWNERS IMPORT CLASSIC WHITE WICKER CHAIRS FROM OTHER ROOMS. THE LACK OF A COVERING DRAWS ATTENTION TO THE BEAUTIFUL WOOD FLOOR.

Above: IF THIS WERE A HOUSE DESIGNED IN THE TRADITIONAL MANNER WITH SEPARATE ROOMS FOR DIFFERENT FUNCTIONS, THE KITCHEN WOULD BE GLOOMY, COMPLETELY CUT OFF FROM SUNLIGHT AND THE LOVELY VIEW OF THE WATER. INSTEAD, THOUGHTFUL PLANNING UNITES THE DINING AREA AND KITCHEN INTO A SWEEP OF UNINTERRUPTED SPACE BRIGHTENED BY WHITE WALLS, PALE WOODEN FLOORING, AND GLAZED FRENCH DOORS THAT LEAD TO A WATERSIDE DECK. TRADITIONAL FURNISHINGS ARE GROUPED IN A COZY ARRANGEMENT ACCESSORIZED WITH DUCK DECOYS, A LIGHT BLUE AND WHITE ORIENTAL-STYLE RUG, A SMALL TABLE FOR DISPLAYING KNICKKNACKS, AND A MIRROR TO MEASURE THE PROGRESS OF THAT SUMMER TAN.

Left: IN THIS OPEN-AIR KITCHEN, LIGHT STREAMS THOUGH AN EXPANSE OF WINDOWS AND INTO THE DINING AREA. A PLEASANT MIX OF STYLES, THE KITCHEN CABINETRY AND BLACK LAMINATE COUNTERS ARE UNABASHEDLY MODERN. A FARM TABLE FOR DINING AND CLASSIC LADDERBACK CHAIRS SOFTEN THE CONTEMPORARY LOOK. THE BLACK AND NATURAL WOOD TONES BECOME THE COMMON THREAD THAT PULLS THE DIFFERENT DESIGN ELEMENTS TOGETHER.

Right: BESIDES CREATING A PLEASING ENVIRONMENT, A WHITE KITCHEN EVOKES A SENSE OF CLEANLINESS. MODERN WORK SURFACES AND APPLIANCES BLEND BEAUTIFULLY WITH CABINETRY TOPPED WITH OLD-FASHIONED CROWN MOLDING. INTERIOR SHUTTERS HELP CONTROL LIGHT LEVELS AND GLARE FROM THE OUTDOORS, WHILE THEY VISUALLY SOFTEN THE OTHERWISE CONTEMPORARY SLIDING WINDOWS. RATTAN CHAIRS REMINISCENT OF THE SOUTH SEAS SURROUND AN OLD TABLE. THE NATURAL FINISH OF THE TABLE LEGS REPEATS ON BOTH THE DINING CHAIRS AND THE BAR-HEIGHT SEATING IN THIS INVITING EAT-IN KITCHEN.

Opposite: OPEN-AIR DINING NEED NOT BE VULNERABLE TO SEARING SUN. OFTEN, THE SOLUTION ENTAILS SIMPLY SETTING ASIDE PART OF A COVERED PORCH FOR SUN- AND STORM-FREE DINING. ACCENTS SUCH AS THE STRIPED DINING-CHAIR CUSHIONS, PATTERNED THROW PILLOWS, AND A FOLIAGE-THEMED TABLE SETTING PUNCTUATE A CLOUD-WHITE COLOR SCHEME AND ECHO THE COLORS OF THE VISTA BEYOND. **Above:** NO MATTER HOW LARGE OR SMALL, A PORCH IS A WELCOME AMENITY AT ANY BEACH HOUSE. IN GOOD WEATHER, IT BECOMES AN OUTDOOR LIVING AND DINING ROOM WHERE THE FAMILY CAN GATHER AROUND THE TABLE TO ENJOY A SIMPLE LUNCH WITHIN SIGHT OF THE SEA. SCREENING THE PORCH IS AN INEXPENSIVE WAY TO KEEP INSECTS OUT AND SMALL CHILDREN IN.

Seaside Sanctuaries

It's surprising how small beach-house bedrooms tend to be compared to the public areas. But there's a logic to it all: in primary homes, family members spend a great deal of time working in their bedrooms—completing homework, paying bills, or reviewing office paperwork. Beach houses, on the other hand, are designed to bring people together to visit, prepare meals, and dine.

There are two strategies to overcome the decorating challenge that small vacation house bedrooms present. The one you choose depends, to a great extent, on your decorating style. In a traditionally decorated bedroom, the most practical approach is to emphasize the small dimensions, creating a sense of coziness. The opposite, making bedrooms seem larger than they actually are, is a hallmark of a sleek contemporary scheme. Either option can result in an appealing, comfortable room, no matter how diminutive.

Small patterns, whether in a wall covering or fabric, visually contract a room. The simplest route to a cozy atmosphere is applying a patterned wallpaper border atop the walls to simulate crown molding. Look for patterns associated with the sea through images and colors. An excellent idea for a child's room is a border with a large-scale pattern of white anchors on a navy blue ground. Reinforce the coziness by selecting one of the "molding" colors for wall paint.

Patterns that bring images of sand and surf to mind abound in fabrics with scenes of the seashore, seashells, large waves, seahorses, crabs, and other forms of marine life. Select fabrics that are as similar as possible in pattern or palette for draperies, bed linens, rugs, lampshades, and any other related items. An excellent wall color is, again, one of those picked from the selected patterns or a soothing creamy white.

Wicker and other light, airy furnishings are other building blocks of the traditional decorating style. To prevent a bedroom from looking too porchlike, select wicker and rattan pieces designed along the lines of traditional

Opposite: As private as can be, this bedroom is a true seaside retreat. Beneath the cooling breeze stirred by the ceiling fan, the adults in the family can sleep late, then indulge in a lazy breakfast on the deck. A minimum of furniture—bed, table, and upholstered bench—make the room seem larger. A few wall-mounted accessories serve as decorative finishing touches.

bedroom furniture. Several manufacturers offer a selection of wicker bed frames, dressers, and armoires as well as the ever-popular chairs.

The traditional bedroom is a fitting place to indulge in fabrics. Mosquito netting above a bed is not only pretty but may also be practical. Bed curtains preserve personal privacy in a shared bedroom. Designers generally prefer linen for this purpose because it gently ripples in a breeze. Diaphanous fabrics are pretty as draperies, bed skirts, and dust ruffles.

Sliding patio doors, walls of windows, and an all-white color scheme are proven ways to visually increase the size of a contemporary-style bedroom, but there are other options that add a sense of drama. Wall cutouts establish interior sight lines, giving a small bedroom a greater feeling of depth. A platform bed, which seemingly hovers above the floor, is an excellent bedroom focal point and is sufficiently prominent to make you forget the feeling of being in a confined space. A platform bed also provides extra storage without sacrificing precious floor space or incurring the additional expense of adding closets.

White remains a favorite contemporary color. For the most part, however, architects and designers are moving beyond the blinding icy whites they formerly preferred.

Above: WHAT BETTER WAY TO ESTABLISH THE CHARACTER OF A BEACH COTTAGE BEDROOM THAN WITH SEASHORE MOTIFS FROM NEAR AND FAR? SALVAGED WOOD COLLECTED WHILE STROLLING ON THE BEACH HAS BEEN RECYCLED AS A SIMPLE, RUSTIC HEADBOARD. AN OLD TRUNK, THE SORT OF TREASURE OFTEN FOUND AT SEASIDE FLEA MARKETS AND THRIFT SHOPS, DOUBLES AS STORAGE AND A BEDSIDE TABLE. **Opposite:** REGARDLESS OF STYLE, SIMPLE BEDROOM FURNISHINGS ALLOW THE EYE TO CONCENTRATE ON THE ARCHITECTURE. IN THIS SEASIDE HIDEAWAY IN KEY WEST, FLORIDA, THE MASTER BEDROOM FURNISHINGS ARE LIMITED TO JUST A FEW PIECES—A PLATFORM BED, A CONTEMPORARY CHAIR, AND SEVERAL SMALL RUGS. THE RICH WOOD TONES OF THE FLOOR, WALLS, AND CEILING LITERALLY SHINE, CREATING A BEAUTIFUL ROOM. FOR ADDITIONAL LIVING SPACE, THE BEDROOM OPENS ONTO A SHELTERED PORCH, WHICH IS FURNISHED WITH BANQUETTE SEATING AND A DRIFTWOOD COCKTAIL TABLE.

The trend is toward softer hues, especially less intense whites. Other popular bedroom color options include pale greens, blues, and yellows, all of which are eminently suited for beach-house decorating.

Older beach cottages usually have little built-in storage space. Until about 1950, houses generally had few closets, if any. Furniture pieces, usually an armoire or another item of cabinetry, provided the bulk of the storage space. Beach-house storage was much more casual, amounting to little more than three or four shelves nailed to a bedroom wall above a hanging rod. As you might expect, many personal items were in plain view.

To get the storage space you need, shop at flea markets for armoires that are old but not valuable as antiques. Then paint or refinish them to coordinate with your decorating scheme. Take a wooden hanger when you shop to ensure that the piece you like is deep enough to hold bulky items. Wicker baskets provide another attractive way of storing extra towels, bathing suits, and other beach-related items. Some newer units are stackable, freeing up floor space. Another strategy in keeping with a traditional decor is a window seat concealing storage space beneath a hinged lid.

Hang rain slickers and similar items on simple wooden pegs available at the local hardware store. Paint them either the same color as the walls or in a contrasting color. A current favorite is zinc, which looks especially nice paired with white. In a bedroom, pegs are versatile storage items. They can hold small net bags to organize

sunscreen, sunglasses, a hat, a paperback, and other small items that are hard to keep track of.

Finally, if your beach house is short on bedrooms, look to the deck as a possible solution. A portion of it can be enclosed as a room or screened in like an old-fashioned sleeping porch. Children usually like sleeping porches because they are open to the cooling ocean breeze and are a suitable substitute for an overnight camping trip. During the day, a sleeping porch is easily converted into a bug-free outdoor living or dining area.

Unless you are willing to invest a substantial sum of money, limit changes in the bath to simple, cosmetic improvements. Fortunately, small, inexpensive changes can have a major effect on the appearance of a bathroom. Whether the look is traditional or contemporary, purchase coordinated—not necessarily matching—towels, shower curtains, and bath mats. To add an unmistakable touch of

for the bath. Add spots of bright color by incorporating simple accessories—seashell soap dishes or toothbrush holders, for example—that strengthen the nautical theme.

Do-it-yourself projects are one option for inexpensive bathroom updates. Install towel bars that coordinate with the bath cabinetry hardware, repaint the walls, lay down a new floor, or put up new window shutters. However, leave big jobs to the professionals. They have the expertise to replace out-of-style surface treatments, re-enamel pretty but worn fixtures or install new ones, and create an all-new look with interior lighting. Period and reproduction faucets in porcelain are made by all of the major manufacturers. Other popular choices include chrome, pewter, and bright brass finishes that will not scratch or become dull. Faucets inspired by antique designs naturally lend themselves to traditional decors. Industrial-style hardware is perfect for contemporary and eclectic baths. Lever faucets are turned on and off with an arm motion instead of the grabbing and twisting motions required by conventional bath hardware. These are just a few of the options for simple, practical beach-house baths.

luxury, buy the thickest towels you can find for both family members and guests.

Choose colors that echo those of the seashore—foam green, sunset pink, pale blue, warm sand, and sunny yellow are ideal. Select one of these as the dominant color

Opposite: A DIFFERENT TAKE ON AN OLD DECORATING STANDBY IS ALWAYS A·PLEASANT SURPRISE. THIS ROOM, OVERLOOKING THE BEACH, ILLUSTRATES THE IDEA OF A FOUR-POSTER BED TENT APPLIED TO AN ENTIRE ROOM. FLOWING TRANSLUCENT DRAPERIES SPANNING CONTEMPORARY WINDOWS CAN BE CLOSED DURING THE DAY TO DIFFUSE THE BRIGHT SUNLIGHT AND OPENED TO THE STARS AT NIGHT. THE SLIDING GLASS DOORS FORMING THE WINDOW WALL CAN BE OPENED TO SEA BREEZES OR CLOSED TO MUFFLE BEACHSIDE SOUNDS. THE CREAM COLOR SCHEME IS A SOFTER VERSION OF THE BRIGHT-WHITE ROOM. **Above:** NOTHING EVOKES THE FEELING OF TRADITION MORE THAN A BATHROOM WITH A CLAW-FOOT TUB. REINFORCING THE OLD-TIME APPEAL OF THIS BATH ARE AN UNPRETENTIOUS LAVATORY, PANELED WALLS, AND SISAL MATTING ON THE FLOOR. A COLLECTION OF SEASHELLS PROVIDES THE PERFECT DECORATIVE ACCENT.

Opposite: WARM WHITE AND A GENEROUS USE OF FABRIC CREATE THE ETHEREAL ATMOSPHERE THAT IS THE HALLMARK OF MANY BEACH HOUSES. WHITE INVITES US TO VISIT, WHILE LIGHTWEIGHT FABRICS CONTINUALLY REARRANGED BY THE BREEZE BECKON US TO STAY. THIS LARGE ROOM SUPPLIES ENOUGH SPACE TO INDULGE IN TWO METAL FOUR-POSTER BEDS AND RELATED DRESSINGS BENEATH A STEEPLY ANGLED CATHEDRAL CEILING. THE FABRICS REPEAT ON THE WINDOWS AS DRAPERIES AND AS UPHOLSTERY FOR THE ALCOVE SEAT, WHICH IS PERFECT FOR CURLING UP WITH A GOOD BOOK. A WICKER CHAIR AND DESK SUPPLY AN EXTRA PINCH OF WHITE. **Below:** THE MAIN FEATURE OF ANY BEDROOM IS THE BED ITSELF. ALTHOUGH TUCKED IN A CORNER, THE HANDSOME WOODEN BED IS THE CAN'T-MISS FOCAL POINT OF THIS COZY ROOM, WHICH IS REMINISCENT OF A SHIP'S CABIN. THE SOFT WHITE WALLS AND CEILING CREATE A SUBTLE BACKDROP FOR THE ANTIQUE QUILT, WHICH PROVIDES THE ONLY COLOR AND PATTERN IN THE ROOM.

Above: THOUGH THIS SOUTH SEAS–INSPIRED ROOM AND ITS FURNISHINGS ARE LARGE, THE DECORATIVE INGREDIENTS CAN BE TRANSLATED INTO SMALLER SEASIDE BEDROOMS. THE OVERALL SOFT LOOK IS CREATED BY THE BOUNTIFUL SUPPLY OF FABRIC ON THE METAL FOUR-POSTER BED. DARK FINISHES HINT OF BRITISH COLONIAL–STYLE FURNISH-INGS. TALL SHUTTERS KEEP OUTDOOR GLARE AT BAY AS A WHITE CEILING FAN CIRCULATES COOL AIR INSIDE THE ELEGANT TWO-STORY SPACE.

Above: THOUGH THE VIEW IS AVAILABLE ONLY IN CONNECTICUT, THE IDEAS IN THIS TRADITIONALLY ROOTED BEDROOM CAN BE APPLIED TO VIRTUALLY ANY BEACH HOUSE. THE SOFT, NEUTRAL COLOR SCHEME IS A FRAME FOR THE GLAZING, WHICH SUPPLIES BLUE AND WHITE ACCENTS THROUGH AN ASSORTMENT OF WINDOWS. FURNISHINGS ARE KEPT TO A MINIMUM SO THAT THE DECORATING DOESN'T COMPETE WITH THE ARCHITECTURAL ELEMENTS. A COMFORTABLE BED AND AN OLD TRUNK ARE ALL THAT'S NEEDED IN A ROOM WITH BUILT-IN STORAGE ABOVE THE BED AND A CONSTANTLY CHANGING "MURAL" TO ENJOY.

Above: THOUGH STREAMLINED AND SPARE, A CONTEMPORARY-STYLE BEDROOM OFFERS A WIDE RANGE OF DECORATIVE DELIGHTS. IN THIS OCEANSIDE MASTER BEDROOM, MINIMAL FURNISHINGS DRAW ATTENTION TO—AND FRAME VIEWS OF—THE COVERED PATIO AND THE BEACH. THE LOWER HALF OF THE GLASS WALL HAS BEEN FROSTED TO PROVIDE A BIT OF PRIVACY WITHOUT BLOCKING THE GOLDEN NATURAL LIGHT.

Left: CREATIVE DECORATING IMBUES THIS OTHERWISE SMALL, CRAMPED CHILDREN'S ROOM WITH THE FEELING OF A SUMMER SLEEP-AWAY CAMP. THE MOST NOTICEABLE ELEMENT, OF COURSE, IS AN ECLEC-TIC COLLECTION OF CORK FISHING-NET FLOATS BOBBING OVERHEAD. THE UNEXPECTED FOCAL POINT ALSO DRAWS THE EYE UP TO THE SLOPED CEILING. NATURALLY FINISHED PINE CLADDING ON THE CEILING IS REPEATED ON THE FLOOR AND WINDOW FRAMES. VIBRANT COLORS AND TWO SPARE SINGLE BEDS IN OAK COMPLETE THIS EYE-CATCHING SETTING.

Below: A CONTEMPORARY COLOR SCHEME CAN FILL A PERIOD-STYLE BATH WITH DECORATIVE VIGOR. TRADITIONAL FIXTURES—A RARE COLUMN-FOOT TUB AND A PEDESTAL SINK WITH A WIDE BASE—WERE RETAINED IN THIS REMODELING AND FRAMED WITH CREAM AND BURNT-ORANGE WALLS. THE STARFISH BALANCED ON THE RIM OF THE TUB VISUALLY LINK THE BATH TO A SHORESIDE LOCATION. THE CHECKERBOARD FLOOR PATTERN, AN OLD IDEA THAT IS ENJOYING A STRONG REVIVAL, IS AN EASY WEEKEND PROJECT. SIMPLY LAY ALTERNATING SQUARES OF BLACK AND WHITE VINYL TILE.

Above: CREATIVE THINKING CAN KEEP DECORATING COSTS DOWN AND YIELD WHIMSICAL RESULTS. IN THIS CHILD'S BATH, THE WALLS ARE PAINTED TWO SHADES OF BLUE—SKY AND SEA—WITH THE ADDED EMBELLISHMENT OF "WAVES." ADORNING THE WALLS ARE TOY-STORE "FISH" THAT FURTHER THE DEEP-SEA THEME. TO SAVE SPACE, THE SINK IS A SMALL-SCALE, CORNER MODEL.

Left: MORE AND MORE, PEOPLE IN TEMPERATE CLIMATES ARE OPTING FOR AN OUTDOOR SHOWER. THIS BEAUTIFUL EXAMPLE ALLOWS THE OWNERS TO SHOWER IN THE OPEN AIR WITHOUT SACRIFICING PRIVACY. WALLS OF BLUE AND SAND TILES ECHO THE COLORS OF THE SHORE AS THEY SHELTER A BATHER FROM VIEW AND WIND. THE BATHING AREA IS PART OF A PRIVATE COURTYARD LOCATED DIRECTLY OFF THE MASTER BEDROOM. **Below:** AN OUTDOOR SHOWER WASHES AWAY SALT WATER AND HELPS KEEP SAND WHERE IT BELONGS. THE DESIGN TENDS TO BE SIMPLE AND STRAIGHTFORWARD BECAUSE THIS TYPE OF SHOWER IS FOR RINSING, NOT BATHING AND GROOMING. THAT DOESN'T MEAN A NICETY SUCH AS HOT WATER CAN'T BE INCLUDED. THIS SHOWER INCORPORATES A VERY SIMPLE SOAP AND SPONGE HOLDER.

A b o v e : THANKS TO A LIGHT-HANDED DECORATING APPROACH, THIS BATH ALMOST APPEARS TO BE A PAINTING INSTEAD OF A ROOM. THE SPARE STYLE RELIES ON ARCHITECTURAL DETAILS TO CREATE A DECORATIVE MOOD REMINISCENT OF AN ENGLISH COTTAGE. THE TUB, WITH ITS BRIGHT BRASS HARDWARE, IS FRAMED WITH PLANKS THAT COMPLEMENT THE WAINSCOTING. AN OLD-FASHIONED-STYLE LAVATORY, WIDELY AVAILABLE IN REPRODUCTION, LENDS THE ROOM A STATELY AIR. DECORATIVE ACCESSORIES HAVE BEEN KEPT TO A MINIMUM—A TUBSIDE WASHSTAND AND A FEW BASKETS TO WARM UP THE WHITENESS.

Accents and Details

If you've ever doubted the old expression "accessories make a room," decorating a beach house will make you a true believer. Being at the beach means being close to the outdoors. And Mother Nature is certain to deliver a potpourri of decorating items—including shells, driftwood, and coastal grasses—literally at your doorstep. All you have to do is collect the most appealing ones and blend them into your seashore decorating theme.

Interior designers tend to plan a room from the floor upward. Floor treatments deserve extra thought because they are subject to drifting sand, dripping bathing suits, and fading from bright sun. The most practical treatment for an attractive floor in good condition is to leave it bare. Flooring in less than perfect shape can be painted in a checkerboard pattern. Stenciling creates a lovely effect that can become a fun family project. For the most part, beach houses and carpeting don't mix. Suitable substitutes are area rugs and floor cloths that can be taken

outdoors and shaken or easily replaced. Natural materials have long been a popular choice for beach-house floors. Selections range from sisal to soft coir and sea grass. They work well in a number of decorating styles and are available in many patterns. Unfortunately, these materials are vulnerable to fading from sunlight, they stain easily, and they are difficult to clean.

Paint is an effective decorating tool throughout the house and has long been synonymous with wall treatments.

Opposite: Even the most fanatic sun worshiper will enjoy tucking into the soft cushions and fringed throw of an old-fashioned rattan chaise such as this. Beautiful curving arm rests and a tightly woven chair back and seat invite one and all to delay that brisk, early morning walk along the beach in favor of sinking back with a hot drink and the latest summer novel. Above: When it comes to the details, this house has it all. Glass walls on both the first and second floors overlook a grand wooden deck. At the center is a beautiful swimming pool for away-from-the-beach parties. Steps lead down to the sandy shore, while a high wooden fence ensures privacy.

While year-round living limits how daring a paint scheme can be, a beach house is a great setting in which to push the creative envelope. White, of course, is always right, but there are many other options. Pale yellows and any number of blues fit easily into a living room. For an eye-catching effect, limit color to one wall. Many designers suggest brighter shades for public rooms and lighter ones for bedrooms and baths.

Spice up a setting by applying a decorative paint treatment. Ragging, sponging, and stenciling are visually intriguing but easy enough to accomplish over a long weekend. Achieving these distinctive and pretty decorative effects requires no special tools. Decorative paint treatments are especially helpful when, as is frequently the case with beach getaways that are second homes, the sale includes the furniture. As long as they are not valuable, old or unfashionable pieces can be visually revived—even made charming—with a decorative finish.

Moldings can be easily implemented to imbue a bland room with architectural character. Adding historic moldings is a common way to bring flair to a traditional ranch-style house. Curved, organic-looking moldings are

Right: DECORATIVE PAINT FINISHES CAN TRANSFORM A WALL FROM A CANVAS TO A WORK OF ART. A STRONG SHADE OF TERRA-COTTA PAINT HAS BEEN VISUALLY SOFTENED AND "AGED" BY SPONGING. BATHED IN LIGHT FROM THE LEADED-GLASS CASEMENT WINDOWS, A LARGE-SCALE MODEL SAILBOAT AND A FLOWER ARRANGE-MENT ADD DECORATIVE VITALITY. A WATERCOLOR OF ANOTHER SAILBOAT FLOATS IN A DRIFTWOOD FRAME.

frequently installed in contemporary homes to soften the stark straight lines associated with this style. Beadboard paneling and moldings are usually painted white or another solid pale color, such as sky blue. Also popular are natural wood finishes. Dark varnishes, standard in earlier times, are too formal and gloomy for the casual, light-hearted atmosphere of a beach house.

Wallpaper adds visual interest to any room and eliminates the expense of purchasing artwork. Combining paint and a wallpaper border can yield interesting results. Placing the border at the top of a wall draws the eye upward, making a large room seem even bigger and visually expanding the proportions of a small one. Wallpaper and paneling are often found in tandem, especially in older, traditionally styled houses. Applied to the lower half or lower two-thirds of a wall, the paneling forms a solid, visual base for the patterned papers above.

Another area ripe for creative self-expression is interior lighting. The local flea market will almost always yield old kerosene lanterns (for display in good weather, or for lighting when storms knock out the supply of electricity) as well as sea-related knickknacks that can be converted into lamp bases. You may even discover a lovely old porcelain table lamp that can be repaired, rewired, and, thus, recycled. While these ideas are tailored for traditional decorating schemes, imaginative ideas for contemporary interiors abound. An antiques shop or flea market may have pairs of wall sconces that can be individually mounted. Equipped with rheostats, they can be

set at various levels to change the mood. Dimmed, they double as hallway night lights for weekend guests.

Outdoor items, such as clay pots, woven baskets, metal watering cans, floral-patterned fabrics, and scented candles, can be brought indoors to great effect. They form the core of what is sometimes referred to as the garden look, an approach that goes hand in glove with traditional decorative schemes. Clay pots and textiles in a limited number fit equally well into a contemporary scheme.

Certain rooms lend themselves to particular accessories. A wall-mounted collection of hats in the entry is a familiar example. To tailor this idea for a beach house, choose fishing and sun hats that you will actually take off the wall and wear outdoors. Local memorabilia in the living room unmistakably identifies your beach house as a vacation retreat. Ask guests to collect pine cones and ferns on their walks. Arrange the pine cones in a bowl; press and mount fern leaves in clear frames. Prints from old books add panache to the living room or bedroom. Mounted in antique or antique-looking frames, they are striking.

Group and place accessories for maximum visual effect. A large collection easily overwhelms a room. Break it up into several smaller arrangements of contrasting heights and place them throughout the house. Dedicate one wall in a living room or stairwell to a portrait gallery accented with framed photographs of beach scenes. Tables, fireplace mantels, the top of a piano, and shelves supply additional display space without requiring you to put holes in the wall.

Above: IN THIS ROOM, VISITORS ARE RIVETED BY THE UNEXPECTED FLOOR TREATMENT. THE CREATIVE PERSON BEHIND THIS DESIGN CHOSE A LINE FROM A CLASSIC SONG AND EDGED IT TOP AND BOTTOM WITH A TWISTED ROPE MOTIF TO FORM THE "BORDER" OF A NONEXISTENT RUG. THE FRAMED PORTION, USUALLY RESERVED FOR THE PRIMARY PATTERN OR FIGURE, HAS BEEN LEFT BLANK TO ALLOW THE COLOR OF THE FLOOR TO SHOW THROUGH. PROTECTED BY A CLEAR SEALANT, THIS IS ONE RUG THAT CAN SIMPLY BE SWEPT CLEAN.

Below: WHILE A BEACH HOUSE SHOULDN'T FEEL CLUTTERED, YOU CAN CERTAINLY DISPLAY A FEW FAVORITE PIECES OF ART. THE TYPE OF ARTWORK IS YOURS TO DECIDE, BUT A BEACH-HOUSE ENVIRONMENT NATURALLY LENDS ITSELF TO NAUTICAL PRINTS, WATERCOLORS, OR AS IN THIS CASE, FRAMED PHOTOGRAPHS SUSPENDED WITH ROPE.

Above: THE SIMPLICITY OF THIS CASEMENT WINDOW COMPLEMENTS THE SERENE VIEW OF WATER AND SAND. THE MODEL SAILBOAT IN THE FOREGROUND SEEMS POISED TO PUT TO SEA. PERCHED ON A LOW CABINET, THE SAILBOAT BOTH EXPRESSES THE OWNERS' PERSONAL INTEREST AND BEAUTIFULLY ACCESSORIZES THE ROOM. AT THE TOP OF THE WINDOW IS ANOTHER EXPRESSION OF THE OWNERS' INTEREST—A COLLECTION OF SEASHELLS.

Left: ECLECTICISM IS OFTEN THE BEST CHOICE FOR DECORATING A BEACH HOUSE THAT MUST PLEASE A CROWD, BUT PULLING IT OFF REQUIRES A GREAT DEAL OF THOUGHT. THIS LIVING ROOM IS ENLIVENED BY THE RICHNESS OF A DAMASK SOFA UPHOLSTERED IN GOLD AND WHITE STRIPES AND COVERED WITH THROW PILLOWS IN THE COLORS OF THE SEA. A SIMPLE CANE TABLE HOLDS A SEA-BLUE DRINKING GLASS AND—WHAT ELSE?—A SAMPLE OF THE MARINER'S HOBBY, A MINIATURE SHIP IN A BOTTLE. **Below:** OUTDOOR CHAIRS, AN UMBRELLA, AND INDEED, THE EXPANSIVE DECK ITSELF ECHO THE DAZZLING WHITE OF CLOUDS AND SAND, MAKING IT A POPULAR DAYTIME RENDEZVOUS FOR SUNNING AND CONVERSATION. AT NIGHT, THE CHAISE LONGUES AND OTHER SEATING ARE PUSHED ASIDE TO MAKE ROOM FOR COCKTAIL PARTIES AND DANCING BENEATH THE STARS.

Opposite: WHITE IS ALWAYS RIGHT AT THE BEACH, ESPECIALLY WHEN IT'S WICKER. PERFECT FOR A SCREENED PORCH, WICKER WELCOMES FRIENDS AND FAMILY TO RELAX AFTER AN AFTERNOON OF SAND AND SUN. "AWNING-STRIPE" UPHOLSTERY ADDS COLOR CONTRAST THAT EMPHASIZES THE PRETTY WHITE FURNISHINGS. A VERSATILE SPACE, THE SCREENED PORCH ALLOWS THE OCEAN VIEWS— AND BREEZES—TO BE ENJOYED FROM A BUG-FREE ZONE.

Left: SOMETIMES THE BEST ARTWORK IN A BEACH HOUSE IS THE VIEW. THAT'S CERTAINLY THE CASE IN THIS HOUSE, WHERE A VIEW OF AN OLD LIGHTHOUSE IS FRAMED BY THE WINDOW. THE LIGHTHOUSE STANDS AS A ROMANTIC REMINDER OF A BYGONE ERA THAT PRECEDED THE DEVELOPMENT OF ELECTRONIC SHIP-TO-SHORE COMMUNICATION. ON A WINDOWSILL, ANOTHER REMINDER OF THE PAST STANDS SENTRY—A DELICATELY PROPORTIONED CLEAR-GLASS KEROSENE LAMP.

Below: IN A STATELY YEAR-ROUND HOUSE, ACCESSORIES RECALL THE DAYS WHEN SUCCESSFUL SHIP CAPTAINS BUILT IMPRESSIVE MANSIONS NEAR THE SEA. FRAMED DRAWINGS ATOP A CHEST REVEAL THE OWNERS' LOVE OF SAILING AND MODERN ART. A HURRICANE LAMP PROVIDES GENTLE LIGHTING FOR AN AFTER-DINNER DRINK WITH FRIENDS.

Above: ARTFULLY GROUPED, MANY DIFFERENT TYPES OF ACCESSORIES REIN-FORCE THE DECORATING THEME AND ENGAGE THE EYE. ARRANGED ON A FIRE-PLACE MANTEL, STARFISH, SHELLS, VINTAGE GLASS BOTTLES, AND BEAUTIFULLY FRAMED PRINTS OF FISH AND OTHER SEA LIFE ARE SURE TO ATTRACT THE GAZE OF GUESTS AND STIMULATE INTERESTING CONVERSATION. **Left:** WITH ACCES-SORIES, SMALL TOUCHES CAN HAVE A BIG EFFECT. FOR AN OCEANSIDE MOOD AT MEALTIME, BORROW A FEW SMALL OBJECTS FROM SHELVES AND TABLES IN OTHER ROOMS TO SCATTER CASUALLY ON THE TABLE. THIS WOULD ALSO BE THE PERFECT PLACE TO USE THOSE PRETTY BEACH DISCOVERIES AS CANDLEHOLDERS. YOU'LL CREATE A MEMORABLE TABLE SETTING WITH VERY LITTLE EFFORT.

Below: THE BEACH IS THE PLACE FOR GETTING BACK TO THE ESSENTIALS. AND THEY ARE HERE: A CLOUDLESS SKY, THE WHITEST OF SAND, REFRESHINGLY COLD WATER, AND A HUGE UMBRELLA TO SHADE THE BEACH CHAIR. FROM THIS COMFORTABLE SEAT, A BEACHGOER IS FREE TO BUILD A SAND CASTLE, DRY OFF FROM A SWIM, READ A BOOK, OR BETTER YET, ENJOY A NAP.

Above: OCEANSIDE LIVING CREATES INTERESTING JUXTAPOSITIONS. A BEAUTIFUL RUSH-SEAT CHAIR STANDS SENTINEL, PATIENTLY AWAITING THE HOME-OWNER TO COME WITH BOOK IN HAND. OR MAYBE THE CHAIR MARKS THE BEST SPOT TO VIEW THE SUNSET. IN EITHER CASE, A SECTION OF AN OLD WALL— OR IS THIS PART OF A WRECKED SHIP?—PROTECTS THE CHAIR FROM BLOWING SAND.

Right: ECHOING THE COLOR AND MOOD OF THE OUTDOOR LANDSCAPE IS AN EASY WAY TO BLEND A BEACH HOUSE INTO THE SETTING. THE STRONG COLORS OF THE SKY, SEA, AND THE SANDY BEACH HAVE BEEN BROUGHT INDOORS VIA A TRUNK, OAK FLOORING, AND A RUG ACCENTED WITH BLUE. A SHIMMERING, TRANSLUCENT WHITE CURTAIN FILTERS STRONG SUNLIGHT WITHOUT OBSCURING THE VIEW. THIS IMAGINATIVE TREATMENT IS MOUNTED ON A ROD RUNNING ATOP ALL THE WINDOWS. WHEN DRAPERY IS CALLED FOR, IT SLIDES ALONG THE ROD TO THE CHOSEN WINDOW.

Outdoor Spaces by the Water

Why do we go to the beach? To enjoy the great outdoors, of course! At a beach house, you have the option of frolicking in the surf or relaxing in the sun without leaving the property. More and more, outdoor spaces geared for fun and relaxation are becoming an integral part of beach-house design. You have many choices for blending indoor and outdoor spaces: a deck, porch, patio, gazebo, and even a sunroom. You can make these spaces even more appealing with the addition of a pool or hot tub.

The best way to decorate an outdoor space is to think of it as a room, albeit one without a ceiling. Indeed, the only difference is that furnishings must be able to withstand inclement weather. What are the dimensions of the space? What purpose will it serve—will it be a secondary living room, dining area, kitchen for grilling, or merely a level, sand-free zone for children's games? By thinking these issues through, you can determine the desired type and amount of furnishings.

Gone are the days when the only outdoor furniture choices were redwood picnic benches or wrought-iron tables. Those are still available, but the selection has widened to include stylish seating in synthetic materials that look like wicker and rattan. Wood and metal are often used together—teak and galvanized steel or aluminum is a favorite combination.

Outdoor pieces by brand-name manufacturers can be supplemented by pieces available at discount outlets and unfinished furniture stores. For sitting and lounging, look at the variety of hammocks, chairs, rockers, chaises, and porch swings now available. Benches made of iron, cast aluminum, and wood are specially made for the garden. French bistro-style round tables and chairs have been embraced by discounters, who sell them at bargain-basement prices. Umbrellas are classic, but shading options have widened to include awnings and draperies, which are often drawn back and tied to columns for effect.

Opposite: CURVING ELEMENTS INHERENTLY HEIGHTEN THE DESIGN INTEREST OF THE RECTILINEAR SHAPE OF TODAY'S HOUSES. A DECK ADDS THAT FLAIR WITHOUT THE EXPENSE OF BUILDING WALLS AND A CEILING. LOOKING MUCH LIKE THE PROW OF AN OLD WOODEN SHIP READY TO HEAD INTO THE BAY, THIS DECK—ELEVATED AND FURNISHED WITH ADIRONDACK-STYLE CHAIRS—IS READY FOR AN AFTERNOON UNDER THE SUN. THE SOLID DECK WALL INCREASES SAFETY FOR CHILDREN.

If your preference runs to the old, search seaside flea markets and secondhand stores for vintage benches, chairs, and tables. Many pieces need only a new coat of paint to look as good as new. Place a bench against a wall or deck railing and sprinkle with colorful cushions to create a banquette. Remodel with fabric. You can buy ready-made slipcovers to fit standard chairs. Or order up a custom set that includes a tablecloth and napkins in the fabric of your choice.

Cushions are a must-have for outdoor furnishings. And like cushions, accessories have moved from the indoors out: floor coverings, slipcovers, handicrafts, and such furnishings as metal baker's racks are all regulars in outdoor living spaces. Pewter, chrome, copper, steel, and aluminum are used for watering cans and other small items. Outdoor lighting in the form of candles, hurricane shades, and metal lanterns is both beautiful and practical. Vibrantly colored, long-lasting plastic tableware is available in beach hues—periwinkle blue, lime green, purple, yellow, and orange. Group these on brightly patterned tablecloths with matching napkins and a candle or two for a fun and casual alfresco meal.

Right: AN ELEGANT BALCONY IS A PICTURE-PERFECT SETTING FROM WHICH TO VIEW GLORIOUS SUMMER SUNSETS. BEFORE GOING OUT FOR THE EVENING, THE OWNERS SAVOR THEIR TIME ON THE BALCONY AS A TRANSITION FROM THE DAY'S WORK. CARVED BALUSTRADES FILTER LATE-AFTERNOON SUNLIGHT AND MORNING BREEZES. THE LOW WALL ALLOWS AN UNIMPEDED VIEW OF THE BAY. IN THIS BAROQUE-STYLE SETTING, FURNISHINGS ARE LIMITED TO SIMPLE METAL CHAIRS AND A SMALL BISTRO TABLE.

Above: A private deck off the master bedroom is a prize amenity. This is where the adults of the house retreat to soak up the sun and the ocean view from the seating of choice—a relaxing wicker chaise longue. Fitted with plump pillows, the chaise is tailored for whiling away an afternoon with a stack of magazines. The deck itself is an island of privacy for enjoying an intimate moment before dinner guests arrive.

Opposite: SUN AND SHADE ENLIVEN THE SIMPLE WOODEN FLOORING OF A SEASIDE DECK THAT LEADS TO A SWIMMING POOL. THE BOARDS ARE SET AT AN ANGLE TO CREATE A SUBTLE PATTERN THAT ADDS A BIT OF DECORATIVE DASH. PROPERLY TREATED, A WOODEN DECK WILL LAST FOR YEARS, DESPITE EXPOSURE TO THE ELEMENTS.

Above: ENCLOSING PART OF A DECK RESULTS IN BOTH AN OUTDOOR AND AN INDOOR ACTIVITY AREA. THE ENCLOSED SPACE, WHICH DOUBLES AS AN INFORMAL LIVING ROOM, IS SIMPLY FURNISHED WITH COMFORTABLE CHAIRS FACING THE WATER VIEW. INCORPORATED INTO THE OVERALL DESIGN OF THE HOUSE, THIS GLASSED-IN AREA SNUGGLES UNDER THE MAIN ROOF. IT IS A COMFORTABLE REFUGE FROM RAIN AND THE OCCASIONAL COLD SNAP WITH AN EXPANSIVE VIEW THROUGHOUT THE YEAR.

Left: THIS UNIQUE HOUSE HAS SEVERAL OUTDOOR AREAS TO ALLOW FAMILY AND FRIENDS TO ENJOY THE REFRESHING SALT AIR AND THE BEAUTIFUL VIEW. UPSTAIRS, A WRAP-AROUND PORCH PROVIDES PRIVACY FOR THAT FIRST CUP OF COFFEE WHEN YOU'RE STILL IN YOUR PAJAMAS. THE SPLIT-LEVEL DECK ENCOURAGES SOCIALIZING OVER A RELAXED MEAL OR BASKING IN THE SUN IN THE COMPANY OF GOOD FRIENDS.

Below: AT THIS BEACH HOUSE, AN OPEN-AIR "WINDOW" IN A WINDBREAK FRAMES A VIEW OF THE OWNERS' PRIVATE HIDEAWAY—A SPRAWLING SUNNY DECK. A SWATH OF WINDOWS IN THE LIVING ROOM ALLOWS GUESTS WHO PREFER AIR-CONDITIONING OVER WARM SUN TO VICARIOUSLY ENJOY THE FUN OF OUTDOOR GAMES AND ACTIVITIES. A PROTECTIVE ROOF OF SEMI-OPAQUE BLUE PLASTIC SHEETING GLOWS IN THE SUN AS IT SHADES THE WEST-FACING WINDOWS AND WALKWAY.

Above: COULD THIS BE THE LONG-SOUGHT "SUGAR SHACK" OF '60S ROCK FAME? IT CERTAINLY LOOKS THE PART WITH THAT SEASIDE STAPLE, VERTICAL BOARD-AND-BATTEN CLADDING, AND A SNACK BAR WITH ACCESS TO THE KITCHEN THROUGH SLIDING WINDOWS. THE DEEP OVERHANG SHELTERS THE INTERIOR FROM THE HOT AFTERNOON SUN THAT FLOODS THE DECK. A STYLISH METAL CHAIR IS COMFORTABLY UPHOLSTERED IN YELLOW AND WHITE STRIPES TO ADD AN EXTRA TOUCH OF COLOR. A ROD BELOW THE SNACK BAR KEEPS TOWELS HANDY FOR A QUICK DIP IN THE OCEAN.

Below: IMBUE AN OUTDOOR SPACE WITH A TOUCH OF THE EXOTIC. REMINISCENT OF PROVENCE, THIS SEASIDE SETTING IS GEARED FOR AN ELEGANT OUTDOOR LUNCH. THE CHAIRS, A FASHIONABLE MIX OF METAL AND WOOD, ARE DRAWN UP TO A DELICATELY PROPORTIONED TABLE. A SMALL UMBRELLA SHADES WHAT LITTLE AREA IS NOT PROTECTED BY THE HOUSE. A THICK AND COLORFUL CARPET OF GREEN GRASS IS ONE OF THE MOST COMFORTABLE "FLOOR TREATMENTS" AROUND.

Above: IN THE FREE-SPIRITED ENVIRONMENT OF THE BEACH, THERE'S ALWAYS AN EXCUSE TO LIGHT UP THE NIGHT. CANDLE-POWERED LANTERNS SUCH AS THESE ILLUMINATE ALFRESCO MEALS, SERVE AS A SOFT BACKGROUND TO LATE-NIGHT CONVERSATION, AND MARK WALKWAYS AND STEPS FOR INCREASED SAFETY. GLASS KEEPS WIND FROM EXTINGUISHING THE CANDLES.

Above: THIS PORTION OF A PRIVATE BEACH IS ZONED FOR DIFFERENT ACTIVITIES. IN THE SUNBATHING AREA, CHAIRS FACE BOTH EAST AND WEST FOR SUN WORSHIPERS IN THE HOUSEHOLD. AN OVERSCALED REFRESHMENT TRAY, WHICH CAN EASILY BE CARRIED INDOORS AT DUSK, SUBSTITUTES FOR A TABLE. A SECOND SEATING AREA IS A SHADY OASIS PROTECTED BY A WALL OF THE HOUSE. IN FULL SUN ARE CHAIRS AND A TABLE FOR SNACKING OR AN INFORMAL LUNCH.

Left: THIS DELICATELY COLORED STUCCO HOUSE CALLS TO MIND THE CLASSIC VILLAS OF SPAIN, WHICH PROFOUNDLY INFLUENCED THE ARCHITECTURE OF FLORIDA, MEXICO, AND THE CARIBBEAN. THIS HOME OFFERS AN EXAMPLE OF THE SPANISH-DERIVED TRADITION OF OBSCURING THE HOUSE AND PATIO FROM STREET VIEW. ANY PASSERSBY SEE ONLY THE OPPOSITE SIDE OF THE WALL. THE WINDOWS FEATURE A PAIR OF OPERABLE SHUTTERS ON EACH SIDE. WITH THE SHUTTERS AND DOORS CLOSED, AS THEY USUALLY ARE, THE ACTIVITIES BEHIND THE WALL ARE HIDDEN FROM VIEW. ONCE THROUGH THE DOORS, THERE IS A SPACIOUS OPEN PATIO THAT ALLOWS THE FAMILY TO ENJOY THE OUTDOORS IN PERFECT PRIVACY.

Left: DINING ON THE TERRACE MAKES PERFECT SENSE DURING SUMMER. WHETHER IT IS A LIGHT LUNCH OR A HEARTY DINNER, EATING OUTDOORS IS A RELAXING CHANGE FROM THE EVERYDAY GRIND. THIS SUNSPLASHED TERRACE REFLECTS A CAREFREE MEDITERRANEAN AIR WITH ITS GRAND STAIRCASE, STUCCO WALLS, AND BRIGHT APRICOT COLOR. FURNISHINGS REFLECT THE LATEST OUTDOOR TRENDS: SCULPTURAL CHAIRS, A TERRA-COTTA TILED TABLE, AND BRIGHT YELLOW NAPKINS.

Right: ONE WAY TO MAKE ROOM FOR ALL THE OUTDOOR ACTIVITIES YOUR FAMILY ENJOYS IS TO TREAT THE SPACE AS ONE LARGE OPEN-PLAN ROOM. IN THIS OUTSTANDING EXAMPLE, THE MOST NOTICEABLE ELEMENT IS THE SWIMMING POOL FOR EXERCISE AND WATER GAMES. TWO AREAS ARE RESERVED FOR LOUNGING— ONE IN THE SHADE AT POOLSIDE; THE OTHER, A SUNNY SPOT "FURNISHED" WITH A HAMMOCK. THE LAWN IS THE SITE OF BADMINTON AND OTHER GAMES. THESE AREAS ARE "SUNKEN," MUCH LIKE SOME LIVING ROOMS, AND REACHED BY STEPS FROM A LARGE AREA RESERVED FOR OUTDOOR DINING.

Above: HAVING A DECK NEED NOT LEAVE YOU OPEN TO VIEW BY PASSERSBY. ELEVATED AND SET BEHIND TREES FOR PRIVACY, THIS RAILED DECK IS A QUIET, SECLUDED SPOT FOR AN AFTERNOON BREAK FROM THE BEACH. BEAUTIFUL WHITE WICKER FURNISHINGS AND BLUE AND WHITE SEAT CUSHIONS CREATE A FESTIVE SETTING. AT NIGHT, THE OWNERS EASILY MOVE THE LIGHTWEIGHT FURNISHINGS INDOORS FOR PROTECTION FROM THE ELEMENTS. **Opposite:** LAND AND SEA MEET IN DESIGN HARMONY AT THIS MODERN, CLASSICALLY INSPIRED HOUSE. GEARED FOR OUTDOOR LIVING, THIS HOME HAS BEEN GIVEN A COVERED FRONT PORCH AND A SITTING AREA DEFINED BY PAIRS OF COLUMNS. AT THE WATER'S EDGE, STONE STEPS LEAD DOWN TO AN EXPANSIVE TERRACE WHERE GUESTS CAN SWIM OR WAIT TO BE PICKED UP FOR A BOAT RIDE. PERHAPS THE MOST UNUSUAL FEATURE, HOWEVER, IS THE WALKWAY TO THE OTHER SIDE OF THE WATERWAY. IN CUTOUT FORM, IT REFLECTS THE STYLE AND ANGLES OF THE HOME'S ROOFLINE.

Left: THE BEST ARCHITECTURE IS A BEAUTIFUL BLEND OF SITE AND STRUCTURE. IN THIS CASE, THE RESULT IS A BATHROOM WITH ACCESS TO A DECK DESIGNED AS A HALF-CIRCLE AND PERCHED DRAMATICALLY ON A ROCKY PROMONTORY OVERLOOKING THE OCEAN. THE BLEND OF NATURAL CONTOURS WITH THE GEOMETRIC APPROACH OF THE DECK DESIGN OFFERS DRAMATIC VISUAL CONTRAST, ALTHOUGH THESE ELEMENTS ARE UNITED BY RELATED EARTH TONES. FURNISHED FOR A DAY OF SUNBATHING, THE DECK WALL IS HIGHER THAN EXPECTED, TO BLOCK STRONG WINDS BLOWING OFF THE OCEAN.

Above: THE FAMILIAR RECTANGULAR POOL HAS GIVEN WAY TO THE CURVES OF ORGANICALLY INSPIRED DESIGNS. LARGE ROCKS AND A BOULDER ENHANCE THE SHAPE AND MAKE THIS POOL SEEM AS NATURAL AS POSSIBLE. FITTING NEATLY INTO THE CURVE OF THE POOL, AN ELEVATED PLATFORM CONTAINS A BUILT-IN HOT TUB AND INFORMAL SITTING AREA. THE JUXTAPOSITION OF THE POOL AND THE SALT WATER BEYOND ENABLE EACH TO REFLECT THE OTHER FOR A DAZZLING VISUAL EFFECT.

Left: HOMEOWNERS HAVE EMBRACED LARGE, WRAPAROUND DECKS BECAUSE THEY SUPPLY EXTRA WARM-WEATHER LIVING AND ENTERTAINING SPACE AT RELATIVELY LOW COST. LIKE THE BOW OF A SHIP, THIS DECK CURVES DRAMATICALLY AROUND MOST OF THE BEACH HOUSE, PROVIDING SUNNY AND SHADY SPACES—AND AN OCEAN VIEW—ALL DAY LONG. RAILINGS KEEP ENTRANCED VISITORS FROM FALLING OVERBOARD. MATCHING PLANTERS DEFINE THE SITTING AREA, WHICH IS SPARINGLY FURNISHED WITH CHAISE LONGUES. **Above:** "WALLS" OF TRADITIONAL, DOUBLE-HUNG WINDOWS FRAME THIS CUSTOM SUNROOM OVERLOOKING THE SEA. THE ROOM IS SO SEAMLESSLY WOVEN INTO THE ARCHITECTURE THAT IT IS HARD TO TELL IF IT IS PART OF THE ORIGINAL DESIGN OR A LATER ADDITION. SURROUNDED BY TALL WINDOWS ON ALL SIDES, THE ROOM OPENS TO THE SEA IN THREE DIRECTIONS TO SOAK UP AS MUCH SUN AS POSSIBLE WITHOUT LOSING SIGHT LINES. THE FOURTH WALL BRINGS SEA VIEWS INTO THE ADJACENT LIVING ROOM.

SOURCES

FIXTURES AND FURNISHINGS

Brown Jordan
9860 Gidley Street
El Monte, CA 91731
(818) 443-8971
Outdoor furniture

Casablanca Fan
Company
761 Corporate Center
Drive
Pomona, CA 91768
(888) 227-2178
Ceiling fans

Ebel Inc.
3380 Philips Highway
Jacksonville, FL
32207-4312
(904) 399-2777
Casual furniture

Ficks Reed Company
4900 Charlemar Drive
Cincinnati, OH 45227
(513) 985-0606
Wicker furniture

Fran's Wicker & Rattan
Furniture
295 Route 10
Succasunna, NJ 07876
(800) 531-1511
*Wicker and rattan
furniture*

Giati Designs, Inc.
614 Santa Barbara Street
Santa Barbara, CA 93101
(805) 965-6535
*Teak furniture, sun
umbrellas, and exterior
textiles*

Lloyd Flanders
3010 10th Street
P.O. Box 550
Menominee, MI 49858
(906) 863-4491
*All-weather wicker
furniture*

Old Hickory Furniture
Company
403 S. Noble Street
Shelbyville, IN 46176
(800) 232-2275
Rustic furniture

Outdoor Lifestyle Inc.
918 N. Highland Street
Gastonia, NC 28052
(800) 294-4758
*Leisure and outdoor
furniture*

Pier 1 Imports
301 Commerce Street,
Suite 600
Fort Worth, TX 76102
(800) 245-4595
*Furnishings and
accessories*

Vintage Wood Works
Highway 34 South
Quinlan, TX 75474
(903) 356-2158
*Wooden doors and
decorative trim*

Winston Furniture
Company
160 Village Street
Birmingham, AL 35124
(205) 980-4333
Casual furniture

ARCHITECTS AND INTERIOR DESIGNERS

(pages 2, 68)
Winton Scott Architects
Portland, ME
(207) 774-4811

(pages 8, 10 top)
Louise Braverman, architect
New York, NY
(212) 879-6155

(page 12, 35)
Barbara Barry, designer
Los Angeles, CA
(310) 276-9977

(pages 15, 45 right,
48 right)
Chris Churchill, designer
New York, NY
(212) 722-2887

(page 16)
Michael Ryan, architect
Beach Haven, NJ
(609) 494-5000

(pages 16, 57)
Brian Healy, architect
Boston, MA
(617) 338-2717

(page 20, left)
Thom Ronselle, architect
Biddeford Pool, ME
(207) 282-6800

(pages 25, 26)
Chatham Home
Planning, Inc.
Mobile, AL
(334) 380-9050

(page 34)
Mark P. Finlay Architects
Fairfield, CT
(203) 254-2388

(page 40)
Thomas M. Beeton, Inc.
Interior Design
Beverly Hills, CA
(310) 247-0325

(page 44)
Mary Drysdale
Drysdale Design
Associates
Washington, D.C.
(202) 588-7519

(page 51)
Steven Holl, architect
New York, NY
(212) 989-0918

(page 52)
Steven Foote
Perry Dean Rogers &
Partners, Architects
Boston, MA
(617) 423-0100

(page 56)
Larry Randolph, designer
East Hampton, NY
(516) 324-9342

(page 58)
Peter Samton, architect
New York, NY
(212) 477-0900

(page 59 left)
A. Neuman, architect
Santa Barbara, CA
(805) 684-8885

(page 69)
Stemberg & Aferiat
Architecture
New York, NY
(212) 255-4173

PHOTOGRAPHY CREDITS

©Patti Corville: p. 10 bottom

©Derrick & Love: p. 56 (Larry Randolph, architect)

©Carlos Domenech: pp. 19 top, 20 right, 29, 54, 62, 63 top, 65; 55 (Edward Garcia-Austrich, designer); 64 (Terry Leet, designer)

Elizabeth Whiting Associates: pp. 24, 28, 31, 33 both, 37 both, 38 left, 39, 42, 50 left, 60 right, 61, 63 bottom, 67

Esto/©Scott Frances: pp. 8, 10 top (Louise Braverman, architect); 9, 41 (Mark Thrift, architect)

©Michael Garland: pp. 40 (Thomas Beeton, designer); 66 (Gary Hansen, architect); 59 left (Andy Neuman, architect)

©Tria Giovan: pp. 7, 18, 23 top, 30, 38 right, 45 left, 46 top, 49 both, 60 left

©Jessie Walker Corporation: p. 47 (Chip Hackley, architect)

©Chris Little: pp. 25, 26 (Chatham Home Planning, Inc., designers)

©James Marshall: p. 7

©David Paler: p. 46 bottom

©Eric Roth: pp. 22; 32 (Kalman Construction, designers)

©Keith Scott Morton: pp. 15, 45 right, 48 right (Chris Churchill, designer); 19 bottom (Victoria Hagan, designer)

©Tim Street-Porter: pp. 12, 35 (Barbara Berry, decorator)

©Brian Vanden Brink: pp. 36, 48 left; 44 (Drysdale Associates, designers); 52 (Steven Foote/Perry Dean Rogers & Partners, architects); 20 left (Thom Rouselle, architect); 68–69 (Winton Scott Architects)

©Paul Warchol: pp. 51 (Steven Holl, architect); 57 (Brian Healy, architect); 16–17 (Brian Healy and Michael Ryan, architects); 21, 58 (Peter Samton, architect); 2, 59 right, 69 right (Stamberg & Aferiat Architects)

©Melanie West: p. 24 (Mark P. Finlay Architects)

©Deborah Whitlaw: pp. 11, 50 right; 23 bottom (Michael Barie, owner/designer)

INDEX